Bob the Alien Discovers the Dewey Decimal System

by Sandy Donovan ∞ illustrated by Martin Haake

PICTURE WINDOW BOOKS
a capstone imprint

Thanks to our advisers for their expertise, research, and advice:

Diane R. Chen, Library Information Specialist
John F. Kennedy Middle School, Nashville, Tennessee

Terry Flaherty, Ph.D., Professor of English
Minnesota State University, Mankato

Photo Credits: The Granger Collection, New York, 7: Photodisc, 14 all:

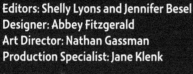

Editors: Shelly Lyons and Jennifer Besel
Designer: Abbey Fitzgerald
Art Director: Nathan Gassman
Production Specialist: Jane Klenk

The illustrations in this book were created digitally.

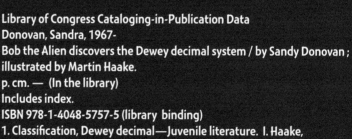

Picture Window Books
151 Good Counsel Drive
P.O. Box 669
Mankato, MN 56002-0669
877-845-8392
www.capstonepub.com

All books published by Picture Window Books are
manufactured with paper containing at least
10 percent post-consumer waste.

Library of Congress Cataloging-in-Publication Data
Donovan, Sandra, 1967-
Bob the Alien discovers the Dewey decimal system / by Sandy Donovan ;
illustrated by Martin Haake.
p. cm. — (In the library)
Includes index.
ISBN 978-1-4048-5757-5 (library binding)
1. Classification, Dewey decimal—Juvenile literature. I. Haake,
Martin, ill. II. Title.
Z696.D7D59 2010
025.4'31—dc22   2009030069

Printed in the United States of America in North Mankato, Minnesota.
032011   006108R

Hi, my name is Allison Wonderland, and this is my friend Bob. He's from Planet Plainold. Bob loves spiders.

Planet Plainold doesn't have books. Bob thought books might help him learn about spiders. Books are great tools to help us learn all sorts of things.

PUBLIC LIBRARY

I took **Bob** to the **library,** a **great** **place** to find **books.**

I BELIEVE

Bob looked around the library.

"Wow," he said. "There are so many books!
How do I find one about spiders?"

"First you need to learn how a library is organized,"
I said. "Then you can find any book."

4

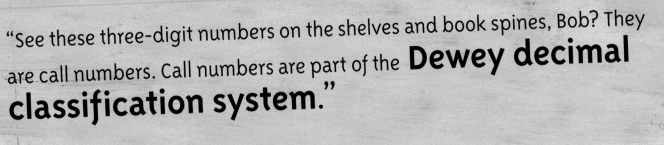

"See these three-digit numbers on the shelves and book spines, Bob? They are call numbers. Call numbers are part of the **Dewey decimal classification system.**"

"Dewey!" Bob said with a laugh. "That's a silly name."

REF 050 New

"Not so silly," I said. "It's named after the man, Melvil Dewey, who invented it. He was a librarian who lived a long time ago."

MELVIL DEWEY,
SECRETARY UNIVERSITY STATE OF NEW YORK.

Before Dewey published his system in 1876, libraries organized their books in different ways. Once the Dewey system became more well-known, almost all libraries used it.

"So how **Dew-ey** do it?" asked Bob.

8

"Every nonfiction book can be put into one of 10 groups. The groups range from the zero hundreds to the 900s. The first number in the call number shows us the group. This book is in the zero hundreds."

"Blee-glop," Bob said.
"Sounds confusing. Can you tell me more?"

group number

REF
050
New

call number

REF
050
NEW

"Sure," I said. "The **zero hundreds** are general books, like encyclopedias. These books have too much information to be grouped into any one subject.

"The zero hundreds also have books that don't fit into other groups. For example, you'll find books about computers and UFOs here."

The UFO - A Complete HISTORY

I kept going. "The **100**s are books about philosophy and psychology. They help people think about feelings and what it means to be human."

"I'd like to know what it means to be human," said Bob.

"Totally," I answered.

I moved on. "The **200s** are books about **religion** and **mythology.** In this group, you can find spiritual and traditional stories," I said.

"The **300s** are books about **social studies.** These books are about how people live and get along together. Books about government are here. So are books about jobs, money, holidays, and the armed forces."

Next I explained, "The **400**s are books about **languages.** In this group you'll find books about the rules of English. Books about foreign languages, such as Spanish and French, are also found here."

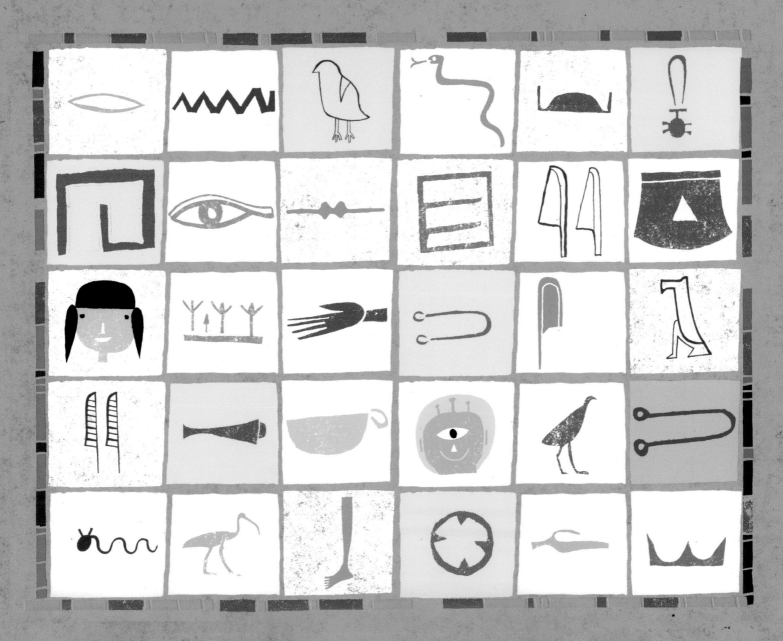

"You can even read about hieroglyphs in this section," I said.

"Hieroglyphs are awesome!"

Bob's brain lights started flashing.

He was starting to understand.

"The **500**s are books about **math and natural science**," I said.
"Natural science is the study of the world around us. That includes
stars, planets, electricity, and volcanoes. It also includes dinosaurs,
rain forests, plants, and animals."

"I love animals,"
Bob said.

"But are we almost done?
I'm getting tired."

600

"Hang in there, Bob," I said. "We also have books about **applied science.** They are in the **600s** group. Applied science is the study of how people use nature to make life easier. In the 600s group you will find books about technology, cooking, health, farming, and cars. Books on secret codes are also found here."

"We're near the end," I said. "We put books about **art and recreation**, or fun activities, in the **700s**. These are books about drawing, painting, and music. Books about sports are also in the 700s."

"**Literature** is in the **800s**. Literature includes stories, poems, and plays. Jokes and riddles are in this group, too. And guess what's last, Bob," I said.

The Dewey decimal system was created to include both fiction and nonfiction books. Fiction books were put in the 800s. But as the number of fiction books grew, libraries ran out of room for the 800s. Librarians moved the fiction books to their own section of the library.

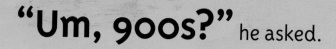

"Um, 900s?" he asked.

"Right!" I said. "The **900**s are books about **history and geography**. If you want to read about explorers, knights and castles, wars, and stuff like that, you look in this group."

000s General books

100s Philosophy and psychology

200s Religion and mythology

300s Social studies

400s Languages

500s Math and natural science

600s Applied science

700s Art and recreation

800s Literature

900s History and geography

"Jeepers!" Bob said. "That's a lot of groups. How do I find spiders?"

"You think spiders hang out in the library, Bob?" I asked.

"Don't be silly," Bob said.

18

I smiled and said, "The hundreds groups just get you to the right part of the library. Remember the numbers on the spine of the book we looked at?"

"The first number tells us which hundreds group the book is in. The 5 means this book is in the 500s. That's the natural science category. The second number stands for a more specific subject. Here, the 9 tells us this book is in the animals group."

595.44
Ram

"My head is **spinning**," Bob said.

He wasn't just saying that because aliens from Plainold can actually spin their heads. He was **confused**.

20

"There's more, Bob," I said. "Let's look even closer. The next 5 is more specific than the first two numbers. This 5 stands for insects and spiders. The last group of numbers puts this book into an even *more* specific group. The 044 means this book is about **tarantulas**. That is a kind of spider."

"Beneath the call number is the first letter or letters of the author's last name," I said. "**Ramirez** is this author's last name."

"What? You have to memorize all those numbers to know where to find any books?" Bob asked.

"No way," I said. "That's what the online catalog is for. Just type in the subject, such as 'spiders.' The catalog gives you the names of books in the library about spiders, along with their call numbers. To find a book, you go to the shelf marked with that call number."

"Oh, here are some!" I said.

"Did you find some spiders?" Bob asked.

"No, Bob," I answered. "But I found eight *books* about spiders."

"Should we check one out?" I asked.

Blee-org!

Sounds good!

Glossary

applied science—the study of using knowledge about the world to make things easier for people

call number—the series of numbers and letters that tells where a book is located in a library; call numbers usually start with one of the 10 hundreds groups.

geography—the study of the earth

government—the group of people who make laws, rules, and decisions for a city, state, country, or organization

history—the study of the past

literature—written works such as novels, plays, and poems that have lasting interest

mythology—a collection of stories that explain the beliefs of a group of people

natural science—the study of how things in the world work

online catalog—a computerized collection of all the books and their call numbers in a library; books can be found in the catalog by searching for titles, authors, subjects, key words, or call numbers.

philosophy—the study of the nature of reality and of how to find truth and knowledge

psychology—the study of the mind, feelings, and human behavior

religion—a system of belief in God or gods

social studies—the study of the ways people live together in different groups

spine—the part of a book's cover that's on the edge; pages are attached to the inside of the spine, and information about the book is printed on the outside.

More Books to Read

Buzzeo, Toni. *Our Librarian Won't Tell Us Anything!* Fort Atkinson, Wis.: Upstart Books, 2006.

Fowler, Allan. *The Dewey Decimal System*. New York: Children's Press, 1996.

Morris, Carla. *The Boy Who Was Raised by Librarians*. Atlanta: Peachtree, 2007.

Vogel, Jennifer. *A Library Story: Building a New Central Library*. Minneapolis: Millbrook Press, 2007.

Internet Sites

FactHound offers a safe, fun way to find Internet sites related to this book. All of the sites on FactHound have been researched by our staff.

Here's all you do:

Visit *www.facthound.com*

FactHound will fetch the best sites for you!

Index

Look for all of the books in the
In the Library series:

* Bob the Alien Discovers the Dewey Decimal System

* Bored Bella Learns About Fiction and Nonfiction

* Karl and Carolina Uncover the Parts of a Book

* Pingpong Perry Experiences How a Book Is Made